SPIRIT
The Way of Wisdom

One man's perspective
of life and how to live it.

SOREN SORENSEN

Published by Spiral Garden

Published by Spiral Garden
www.SpiralGarden.com

ISBN: 978-0-9858237-1-9

First Edition
Published July 2012
Printed on demand by CreateSpace

DEDICATION

This book is dedicated to all that is,
all that has been, and all that will ever be.

May we all experience ever-greater happiness forever!

To this end, a portion of all proceeds will be used to establish
and nurture the Center for a Better World and its projects.

www.CenterForABetterWorld.com

CONTENTS

MEDITATIONS

HOW TO READ THIS BOOK

This is not the kind of book that can be accurately understood by reading from it casually or at random. At least not until you have read it *at least once* carefully from cover to cover. Every chapter of this book builds upon the previous chapter in order to effectively and efficiently share a profound perspective of "life and how to live it". You are invited to use the many blank pages in this book as an opportunity for inner reflection and/ or note taking. *You will be well rewarded for your investment!*

ACKNOWLEDGMENTS

I would like to acknowledge and appreciate, with the whole of my being, all past, present, and future wisdom teachers, both celebrated and forgotten, who have offered a portion of their lives to share the essence of what I, too, attempt to share within these pages. It has never been an easy or welcome task, as one must encounter the inertia of ignorance. Fortunately, it seems as though a worldwide awakening is *finally* near at hand!

Introduction

WHERE IS THE WISDOM?

As I observe the leaders of our world by randomly reviewing news articles, reports, and documentaries, I can't help but wonder, **"Where is the wisdom?"**

One thing is certain - it does not *appear* to be present in the thoughts, words, and actions of the majority of the leaders of our world's most influential businesses, governments, and religions. Or in the leadership of the major media, marketing, promotion, and ad agencies. Or in the membership of the prominent "think tanks" that serve the ambitions and enterprises of all of the above.

In fact, beyond a profound lack of wisdom, it initially *seems* as though many members (leaders and followers alike) of our human family are suffering from an extremely serious and Earth-life (and beyond!) threatening mental disorder! But deeper observation and consideration suggests that, perhaps, the condition is not actually a mental defect as much as it is simply a series of fundamental and critical misunderstandings. Misunderstandings that remain undisturbed and uncorrected as long as one's natural intelligence remains unawakened; stuck unnecessarily in the rut of cultural beliefs (including those of the so-called mystical secret societies), personal habits, and other patterns.

I often reflect on the popular adage, "knowledge is power". I challenge this suggestion. From my point of view, *intelligence* is power. *Knowledge is leverage.* That is to say, that knowledge merely amplifies the power of intelligence. And if "a little knowledge is a dangerous thing", then surely we will all benefit from continuing to expand our fundamental library of knowledge.

This book intends to contribute to the correction and increase of our collective fundamental understanding, while stimulating the awakening of our collective intelligence. My hope is that ever-increasing wisdom will be a natural result.

Ultimately, my dream is to see bona-fide wisdom become the quality most highly sought after and valued in every position of leadership throughout the world.

Of course big dreams require great clarity, therefore I am compelled to define "wisdom" for the purposes of my dream as well as for this book in general.

If intelligence is the ability to personally acquire and apply knowledge for *any* purpose, then wisdom is the ability to personally acquire and apply knowledge for the purpose of *improving one's own health and happiness.*

If this definition of wisdom sounds like a great example of what some have concluded to be one of our world's primary problems, I urge you to read this book very carefully. Perhaps more than once. Because nothing could be further from the truth. *We are one!*

PART I

ATHEISM

Chapter 1

THE NATURE OF WORDS AND NAMES

Why do you stare at my finger
when I point to the moon?

Before we can effectively and efficiently explore the incredibly sensitive, and potentially explosive, topics that are necessarily part of the landscape of atheism, we must understand a few extremely important things that are often overlooked by many well-meaning philosophical adventurers.

First, we must understand that words, terms, and names are merely symbols that refer to other things. *They are not the thing to which they refer!*

Secondly, we must understand that many, if not most, words are used to refer to several different things which range anywhere from slightly different to completely unrelated.

Thirdly, we must understand that dictionaries do not exist for the purpose of providing or proclaiming truth. (Although plenty of truth can, indeed, be found and synthesized within its pages!) Instead, dictionaries exist merely to provide and proclaim the *most popular uses* of particular words by particular people in particular places at particular times. It doesn't matter how official, approved, or accepted a dictionary is; it is still just an attempt to capture and record how a word or term is (or was) used (spoken and written) by people.

Finally, we must understand that the meaning of a word (the referential assignment of a word) cannot be permanently fixed. Or, to be more accurate, the meaning of a word (a word's use) cannot be enforced. People can, and do, use words however they want. And when enough people are in alignment, dictionary editors are expected to *somehow* determine that the required validity has been established and make the necessary adjustments. Of course, this cannot be enforced either!

Keeping all of these things in mind, perhaps we can avoid, or at least significantly minimize, some of the more common communication and comprehension problems that would otherwise threaten to prevent or seriously distort this important sharing of ideas.

Chapter 2

DEFINING
"ATHEIST" AND "GOD"

What is it, exactly, that you don't believe in?

The next order of business is to firmly establish what the term "atheist" means, for the purposes of this book.

According to the (concise) Oxford English Dictionary, "atheism" means "the theory or belief that God does not exist".

This definition provides us with a place to start, but for our inquiry, we need to be *much more specific*.

To that end, and for the purposes of this book, I am going to define the term "atheist" in three progressively more specific ways. Each of them will be valid; but each will be increasingly more specific, and therefore, increasingly more useful for our present purposes.

1) In harmony with most popular dictionaries, "atheist" means "one who believes that God does not exist".

Of course this definition doesn't mean anything technically useful unless we also take the time to clearly define the term "God". *(It is shocking to me how often traditional atheists don't bother to do this. Instead it seems as though an irrational disease rife with understandable emotional baggage has poisoned many potentially powerful minds, manifesting itself as an irrational allergy to the very sound of the term "God"!)*

So what, exactly, does the term "God" refer to?

If we irrationally decide to include any/all possible definitions of the word "God", we necessarily prevent and negate any/all meaningful investigation and discussion; so we must choose, or create, one that sincerely seems most relevant and powerful. *(Again, I am shocked by how often traditional atheists cling, sometimes violently, to the irrational and ultimately fruitless position of insisting upon an all-inclusive definition of/for the term "God"!)*

To illustrate my point, if someone chooses to define "God" as the universe itself (as many people do); then, in that specific case, I believe in the existence of "God" (the universe), which would make me a (non-literal) "theist" according to that specific definition of "God". But if someone chooses to define "God" as a white-bearded wizard who lives just outside of the known universe (as many people essentially do); then, in that specific case, I do not believe in the (literal) existence of "God", which would make me an "atheist" according to that specific definition of "God".

Naturally, each is free to choose his/her own definition of the term "God", but spiritual atheists tend to choose the one that most firmly establishes the quality of atheism while intentionally drawing attention to the gross misunderstanding of traditional lay theists - namely that the term "God" refers to *an entity who exists outside of the universe, and who created and rules the universe.*

Therefore, for the purpose of clarifying atheism, the term "God" is here defined as "an entity who allegedly exists outside of the universe, and who allegedly created and rules the universe" (feel free to picture a white-bearded wizard).

Remember, to be of any real value, we must assign the term "God" to something *specific.* In this case, we have assigned it to the (mythical) creating, commanding, punishing, rewarding, and loving God who is promoted, worshipped, and feared by traditional theists. Now that this assignment has been made, I can restate our definition of "atheist" more precisely in order to give it more value.

2) "Atheist" means "one who does not believe in the existence of an entity who allegedly exists outside of the universe and who allegedly created and rules the universe".

But we must go even further than this in our well intended inquiry!

I am sure that it is obvious to many readers that our mass conception of the mythical white-bearded wizard is itself a symbolic reference to something else.

Sometimes we need symbolic devices that are more powerful than words in order to think and communicate more effectively and efficiently.

It is my belief (as well as the belief of many other spiritual atheists and non-literal theists) that the mythical white-bearded wizard (to whom the term "God" here refers) is one such example, if not the most important example. (Which is followed immediately by "self". More on that later.)

If you are a traditional lay theist I urge you to consider the possibility that your conception of God may actually be a powerful symbol (a "false god", if you will) that ultimately represents something else far more profound.

I propose (I realize that I am, thankfully, not alone in this proposition!) that the mythical white-bearded wizard is a symbolic reference to the universe itself, when conceived as a whole.

This understanding allows me to present an even more valuable definition of the term "atheist" for the purposes of this book, *especially as it relates to spiritual atheists.*

3) "Atheist" means "one who does not mistake the word/term/name/symbol 'God' for that which it refers to, or represents, *which is the universe itself".*

Chapter 3

A BETTER WAY
TO DEBATE

God is in the Details

Before we continue to build upon the ideas so far presented, I want to briefly urge every atheist and every theist in the world who ever engages in any kind of discussion or debate about the existence or non-existence of "God" to first and foremost agree on a *very* specific meaning of the word "God" for the purposes of that specific discussion or debate. And then, if at all possible, leave the term "God" out of the discussion or debate altogether in order to avoid confusion.

If intelligent and well-meaning people would do this one simple thing, wisdom would naturally arise and begin to heal the world in many of the ways it is so sorely needed. In fact, it is my opinion that innocent ignorance in combination with the widespread personal and cultural need for deep emotional healing relating to

"God", religion, etc. is the only thing that really separates science and spirituality.

Let's work together to bring a wise end to this incredibly distracting and destructive debate, so that we can put our combined genius and all other resources to far better uses!

Chapter 4

SUPERNATURAL
BELIEFS

Nature Reveals Her Nature

Do spiritual atheists believe in the supernatural?

This is often a burning question for those new to the topic. In order to answer this question clearly, we must, once again, begin with some fundamental conversational definitions *for the specific purposes of this book.*

"Universe" means "everything that exists".

If you believe that something exists outside of the universe, you are simply arguing with my *definition* of "universe" and nothing more. Parallel universes, alternate realities, realms of lower or higher frequencies or vibrational rates, and any and every other possibility is included within my definition of universe. Just be sure to remember that a possibility is not necessarily a certainty.

"Supernatural" means "that which violates the nature of the universe".

This is a concept born of ignorance. Nothing can *violate* the nature of the universe. All such supposed behavior only further *reveals* the nature of the universe. Hopefully there will always remain some unsolved mysteries. Fortunately, since the universe is infinite, it is a certainty.

So, do spiritual atheists believe in the "supernatural"?

Absolutely not.

Chapter 5

PERSONALITIES

By what name shall I refer to all that you claim to be?

The universe has a PERSONALITY!

If you observe carefully, you will find that all things in the universe have a personality. You, your pet cat or dog, your favorite automobile, your local community, your geographical location, and even your new shoes. The personality of a thing is made up of its qualities, tendencies, etc. The universe is no different.

On a considerably smaller scale, consider the personality of our own planetary home. We have even given it a name - several actually - Earth, Gaia, Pachamama, Mother Earth, Mother Nature, etc.

Is Earth a conscious being or just a thing that has certain qualities and tends to behave in certain ways?

What about you?

Whether you, Earth, and/or the universe are conscious or not, does not change the fact that all of these delineated things have qualities, tendencies, etc. that give them a personality. *If you refuse to acknowledge this, then you limit your own unfolding understanding and wisdom.*

Take a moment to realize and understand that the many culturally specific names of "God" are simply the varied personal names that have been given by our various ancestors to the universe itself. And, of course, there are similarly the lessor "Gods", or aspects of the universe.

If fact, if I remember correctly, some have even called the wind "Mariah"! *What a beautiful name!*

( )

PART II

SPIRITUALITY

SPIRITUAL ATHEISM

Chapter 6

THE FLOW OF
CAUSE AND EFFECT

Free Will is an Illusion

For the purposes of this book, I would like to propose the use of two terms in an unusual way.

1) Outer Space:

> That which you observe outside of yourself
> (everything observable with the five senses)

2) Inner Space:

> That which you observe within yourself
> (emotions, thoughts, conclusions, decisions, etc.)

Outer Space Observations:

When you observe that which takes places outside of yourself (in outer space), do you observe anything that you *honestly* believe is without cause? I propose that nothing you will ever observe in outer space is without cause, regardless of whether or not you are able to identify any of the major causes. And I further propose that all observed events are both a result of an infinity of previous causes as well as a partial cause of other forthcoming results, regardless of whether or not you are able to observe and quantify them.

Inner Space Observations:

For the vast majority of my life I have been observing that which takes place inside of myself (my emotions, thoughts, conclusions, decisions, etc.), and I have yet to observe any occurrence that I truly believe has no cause. Even flashes of intuition (which I do very often experience) seem to me to have causes, whether coming from deep within my own self or from other, more mysterious (less understood), sources in the universe.

I should also point out that the flow of cause and effect moves freely between the two realms of inner and outer space. For instance, if you experience something in the outer world that displeases you, then you are very likely to feel badly inside; if you feel badly inside, then you are very likely to say and do things that will negatively impact the world around you. *And so on.*

Of course, if you are aware of this natural tendency (consciousness is a cause), you may (there are many factors/causes involved) attempt to remain undisturbed by that which threatens to displease you, and instead, be an intentional source of positivity. But this other possible course of events only further substantiates my proposition: there are always specific reasons that things are the way they are, even if they are innumerable, incomprehensible, and/or unimaginable.

So... *where is the "free" will?*

I was in my late teens when I decided to put my own mind to the task of seriously answering this invaluable, yet seldom seriously asked, age-old question. Within a matter of moments I reluctantly concluded that belief in free will is a serious misunderstanding and a grave mistake. The last twenty something years of additional life experience have only strengthened my initial conclusion.

From my point of view, the idea that an emotion, thought, conclusion, decision, etc. could ever be technically independent of the infinite and eternal flow of cause and effect goes against all available evidence.

For the benefit of all who are seriously considering my point of view, I would like to emphatically state that I do not believe that anything or anyone could have ever done, is presently doing, or will ever do anything differently than what they have done, what they are doing, or what they will do. Instead, I believe that everything in the world, including sentient beings, is inescapably bound in (part of) the infinite and eternal flow of cause and effect at every scale. (I do, however, recognize that it is possible for one's awareness to become so great that it becomes an *apparently* unbound (miraculous) cause, but this *illusion* is only a further demonstration of the points that I am herein making.)

I realize that giving up the belief in free will may initially seem pessimistic, and potentially devastating, to many people; but, ultimately, this great truth is incredibly revealing, liberating, inspiring, and empowering.

In the rest of this book, I will teach you how and why.

For now, please just take a moment to seriously consider the potential implications and possibilities that might exist if what I say is true. For instance, if my proposal is correct, it would mean that not only is free will an illusion, but that true independence is also an illusion. Ultimately, it would mean that, as many spiritual and wise beings have proclaimed for centuries, we really are all *one*, in a mystical, mundane, and very practical way.

Chapter 7

THE LIMITATIONS
OF SCIENCE

Science is the Study of God

Occasionally, people will put forth the idea that recent scientific discoveries (e.g. "Quantum Entanglement") somehow prove (or at least suggest) that free will exists; since the quality of one's intentions, observations, and measurements can sometimes have an *apparently* simultaneous affect upon the quality of something else - and possibly even something else that is somehow mysteriously connected to that! I do not see this as proof of free will.

Instead, I would like to argue that if the simple act of intending/observing/measuring something changes it and/or anything else, then intention/observation/measurement, too, is simply a cause in the infinite unfolding of things, as described in the previous chapter. And if things *appear* to be simultaneous, it may simply be an illusion created by our incredibly limited (in comparison to infinity) observational resolution (in terms of both time and space).

There can be little doubt that science will continue to create ever more accurate observational and measurement tools, but infinite resolution will never be attained. Measurement is inherently finite, while the universe is *inherently infinite*.

Also, I would like to point out that the more precise science attempts to be in its observation and measurement of things, it must necessarily give up some of its accuracy of space measurement for better time measurement and give up some of its time accuracy for better space measurement. This is because it takes time to measure space, and space to measure time.

This means that, when observing things outside of the now/here center point of observation (referred to as "outer space" in the previous chapter), we can know where something is or when something is; but we cannot know both with precise accuracy. Understanding this reveals that any one thing moving sufficiently fast could actually *appear* (visually, physically, or otherwise) to be two or more separate things in two or more separate places at the same time - an illusion made possible only by an observer's limited observational capabilities!

With this in mind, I would like to *playfully* propose that if there was an infinitely small particle that could move infinitely far, infinitely fast, it could be responsible for the existence of the entire universe!

Of course, I don't believe that particles really exist as such. Instead, I believe that particles are simply accumulated experiences (observations) of the presence of identifiable energetic states that recur at particular intervals (frequencies), thereby creating recognizable patterns. And if you are able to experience (observe) any aspect of these patterns, then your sensory (observational) intervals (resolution) for a specific energetic state experience (measurement) must be harmonious to the frequency of the experienced (observed) pattern; otherwise, they would remain unexperienced (undetected) - as if in another world that is invisibly interwoven with our own.

I'd like to share one final thought on observation and measurement. If now/here is always the very center of present reality for any given observer, then one can observe and measure the past simply by traveling faster than the energetic aspects of the past that one wishes to review. For instance, if one wanted to go back in visual history (light), one would need to travel faster than its speed (the speed of light). In this case, one would naturally observe (experience) the visual aspect of the past simply by outrunning the radiating energetic evidence. It is the same for audio history (sound), except that one wouldn't need to travel nearly as fast. Naturally, one could travel into the past history of all other radiations in the same manner.

I think the popular notion that "if you could travel faster than the speed of light you would go back in time" (in an absolutely literal, complete, and total way), is simply a misunderstanding and misapplication of *relatively* complicated math. You can't escape now/here. Wherever you go, it comes too.

Considering these suggestions and endless other extraordinary perspectives, positions, and possibilities that might be imagined by other imagining beings (including you!), how could any intelligent being not think of the universe as both infinite and mysterious?

Chapter 8

OUR ULTIMATE IDENTITY

A Wholistic Perspective

If God refers to all that is, then self refers to any part of that whole, especially as experienced by that part.

But what happens if a part's personal conscious awareness expands beyond its immediate physicality?

As one's personal conscious awareness expands, so does one's most intimate sense of self until, finally, one's sense of self potentially includes all that is. This is because self is a referential identity that is relative, and therefore, *scalable*.

Every community is itself a self, and yet, it is made up of individual human (and other) selves, regardless of whether or not they recognize themselves as a part of the larger community. It is the same within one's own body.

What happens if an individual cell fails to understand and act in accordance with its relationship to the whole body?

We call it cancer. And in ignorance, cancer will destroy the very body that makes its own continued life experience possible. Obviously, it is the same in communities (whether international or local); only we call it greed, which is a result of similar ignorance.

In the end, I think it is most powerful to think of one's ultimate identity as being *both* an individual part of the universe that one finds one's self conscious of, as well as being the collective universe itself (or on a currently more practical level, Earth).

Make no mistake - you are an extremely significant part of the whole, and you are at the very center of all that is and all that you will ever experience!

Chapter 9

OUR ULTIMATE
MOTIVATION

Inescapable Selfishness

If you observe long enough, you will no doubt conclude (as so many others over the ages have) that that which psychologically motivates all sentient beings is nothing more or less than the pursuit of personal pleasure, sometimes manifesting as the attempt to avoid personal pain.

Is it possible to be personally motivated by something other than the preservation and expansion of one's own personal pleasure?

I argue that it is not.

Look deeply into your own innermost motivations and you will be able to verify that even the most hopeful candidates for altruism reveal, instead, the subtle motivation to personally experience certain pleasurable things (or avoid certain painful things); and sometimes to personally experience being perceived in certain positive ways (or avoid being perceived in certain negative ways), which is simply a specific manifestation of the same motivation.

The most mystical example of the pursuit of personal pleasure might be the spontaneous and automatic impulse to risk one's own life to save another's. Even then, I would argue that at the subconscious level (which is the level from which a spontaneous and automatic risk of one's own life is most likely to originate from), we are all fundamentally aware of our inherent oneness. Furthermore, for many people this is a consciously nurtured awareness that manifests itself in daily life.

And it must be remembered (from the previous chapter), that self identity is both relative and scalable. First, a man may only be consciously concerned with his own well being. Then, he may marry and become equally concerned with his wife's well being. The birth of their children will likely only further expand his sense of self as his family continues to grow. And as he watches his children grow, his conscious awareness may extend to the far reaches of our planetary home. Eventually, he may even come to realize that, ultimately, we are our children. And all of life everywhere.

Perhaps this is what motivates certain monks and nuns to dedicate their entire lives to the sole task of seeking non-suffering, peace, happiness, etc. (all of which are forms of pleasure) for their individual self as well as for their collective self (the community, the world, the universe, the oneness, etc.). Naturally, one's understanding, perspective, and sense of self is reflected in one's approach to self satisfaction.

We are life itself. And, naturally, we want only for our own happiness.

Chapter 10

THE KEY TO UNHAPPINESS

Fear and Resistance

What is unhappiness?

For the purposes of this book, unhappiness refers to a state of mind that is generally characterized by the following (or similar) qualities:

afraid, angry, blaming, closed, cold, complaining, confused, conniving, controlling, cruel, cynical, defensive, depressed, disconnected, discouraged, disempowered, dishonest, dissatisfied, distrustful, fearful, forceful, guilting, hateful, impatient, inflexible, irritable, jealous, mean, manipulative, negative, ornery, paranoid, pessimistic, powerless, resistant, restless, sad, shaming, stingy, suspicious, tense, tight, tyrannical, unloving, unlucky, ungrateful, uninspired, victimized, worried, etc.

Naturally, one in an unhappy state of mind will not necessarily experience all of these qualities at the same time, but they do tend to enjoy each other's company immensely. Thus, to the unconscious and unhappy person comes even more unhappiness - and quickly!

People commonly believe that they are unhappy because certain undesired things have happened. From my point of view, an opposite proposal is far more accurate (and useful): undesired things tend to happen (much more frequently) when a person is unhappy.

For this reason, I often refer to unhappiness as the *unfortunate (or victimized)* state of mind.

What is the cause of unhappiness?

Unhappiness arises when one resists what one perceives to be, or believes to be, true and is greatly intensified if one refuses to accept truth and allow it to be true. Ultimately, the greater the resistance, the greater the unhappiness.

So... if you want to feel really, really authentically unhappy, simply focus all of your attention on those things that you most wish were different than they presently are and increase, as much as possible, your resistance to accepting and allowing the truth to be as it appears to be! Let yourself feel as resistant, bitter, angry, sad, depressed, etc. as you possibly can!

And learn this lesson well!

What is the solution to the problem of unhappiness?

I prefer not to think of unhappiness as a problem that should be solved. Instead I make the strong suggestion that just as unhappiness is caused, so is happiness. *And the consciousness of this fact is an important aspect of the enlightened cause of happiness!*

Read on!

Chapter 11

THE KEY TO HAPPINESS

Love and Acceptance

What is happiness?

For the purposes of this book, happiness refers to a state of mind that is generally characterized by the following (or similar) qualities:

accepting, allowing, appreciative, calm, confident, connected, courageous, ecstatic, encouraged, empowered, faithful, fearless, flexible, forgiving, fortunate, generous, grateful, happy, honest, inspired, kind, loving, lucky, open, optimistic, patient, playful, peaceful, powerful, relaxed, satisfied, trusting, warm, etc.

Naturally, one in a happy state of mind will not necessarily experience all of these qualities at the same time, but they do tend to enjoy each other's company immensely. Thus, to the conscious and happy person comes even more happiness - and quickly!

People commonly believe that they will be happy when certain desired things happen. From my point of view, an opposite proposal is far more accurate (and useful): desired things tend to happen (much more frequently) when a person is happy.

For this reason, I often refer to happiness as the *fortunate (or empowered)* state of mind.

What is the cause of happiness?

Happiness is the natural result of accepting and allowing that which is true to be true. The less resistance you have to the truth, the happier you will feel. And the more authentic appreciation and gratitude you have for what you believe to be true, the deeper your happiness will be.

So... if you want to feel really, really authentically happy, simply focus all of your attention on those aspects of your life, and life/truth in general, that you are the most genuinely grateful for and increase, as much as possible, your appreciation of those things! Let yourself feel as peaceful, appreciative, happy, fulfilled, ecstatic, etc. as you possibly can!

And learn this lesson well!

Chapter 12

THE KEY TO
HEALING

Release All Negativity

You can't change the truth. You can't change anything that has ever happened; you can't change anything that just now (already) happened; and you will never be able to change anything that will ever happen in the future (once it has happened). In fact, we call the truth "the truth" simply *because* it cannot be changed.

Those things that may or may not happen, but have not yet happened, are simply possibilities (often experienced as hopes and fears); they are not truth and should not be treated as such. Of course, the *presence* of hopes and fears (and any/every other emotion, thought, etc.) is a very important part of what is true. In other words, if you are afraid that something might happen (or might not happen), it is true that you are afraid and it is true that your fear will be a *partial* cause of whatever will become true in the future.

When we experience the truth as being something other than what we would prefer, we either accept it as it is and make the best of our circumstances; or we resist the truth and demand that it change, often by attempting to make someone or something feel badly about itself (fabricating blame, shame, and guilt) in a vain attempt to coerce the truth to change. *But the truth will not be changed!*

In the earlier case (acceptance), we do not create energetic/emotional injury to ourselves. But in the later case (resistance), we create energetic/emotional injury to ourselves. Injury which, if we are lucky, we will later have an opportunity to resolve through the process of "healing".

If you find yourself confused (or possibly even irritated) by metaphysical healers', teachers', and others' use of the word "energy", then just substitute the word "emotion" and you will go a long way towards understanding what they are talking about. It doesn't completely capture it, but the essence is there.

For instance, an "energy block" can also be thought of as "emotional baggage". Either way, releasing the block or dropping the baggage is your key to healing!

Fortunately, there are an endless number of creative and valid healing methods, processes, and paths that can lead to this extremely valuable outcome. Choose whatever path feels most comfortable to you and don't worry about what feels most comfortable to others.

With this attitude in mind, I would like to offer a personal healing meditation that I have developed and used over the years while working with clients. It has proven to be extremely effective if undertaken seriously.

SOREN'S HEALING MEDITATION

First, put yourself in a comfortable and relaxed posture that you can enjoy for an extended period of time. Then, take a few deep breaths and get as comfortable and as relaxed as you possibly can while staying awake and alert. When you are ready, begin to review your own life experience, working backwards from the present moment towards your birth (and potentially, beyond).

For each memory that arises, notice if there is anything about the memory that makes you feel any unhappiness (as defined in chapter 10). If there is, complete the following process as seriously and sincerely as possible.

1) Notice the difference between the facts you honestly believe to be true and those you are not actually sure of.

2) Decide to accept all that is true as being true, simply because it is true. You don't have to approve of it or be happy about it; just accept that which is true as being true.

3) Decide to allow all that is true to be true, simply because it is true and does not require your permission to be true. Again, this does not mean that you approve of it or are necessarily happy about it; just that you are, perhaps finally, allowing that which is true to be true.

4) Decide to forgive everyone (including yourself) and everything (whether apparently living or not) that had anything to do with causing the truth to be true. Work through this process as necessary. (Want to know the biggest and most powerful secret to forgiveness? Read part II of this chapter! But don't skip ahead just yet!)

5) Decide to send a personal blessing to everyone (including yourself) and everything (whether apparently living or not) that had anything to do with causing the truth to be true. This blessing should, at the very least (you can be as elaborate as you like), be an absolutely sincere wish that the recipient may be able to experience anything and everything that he or she wishes in this life and beyond. Be sure not to include any conditions or restrictions. And, of course, be sure to include yourself in this very important distribution of well wishes!

6) Verify that there is no more negative energy to release, no more emotional baggage to drop; and then feel the deep inner sense of relief, lightness, and brightness that is growing stronger and stronger with your every breath and your every energetic/emotional release!

Repeat this powerful process as necessary* until you feel little to no negativity about any aspect of your life. Allow yourself to enjoy your ever-lighter sense of being. *And let yourself become filled with ever-greater joy for every reason you can think of, and possibly, for every reason you can't!*

*This process may take hours, days, months, or even years. And just when you think you are finally finished, you may be sorely reminded that there is even more work to be done. This is not a problem. It is simply the truth. And it is the key to your freedom. If you get stuck along the way, please seek help from a trusted healing professional. *It may, initially, be a bit uncomfortable to do this, but it is far beyond worth it!*

Chapter 12
Part II

FORGIVENESS

There is only Innocence

Unfortunately, in our present day and age, a chapter on healing would be incomplete if it didn't specifically address the topic of forgiveness.

First, I would like to state that the idea of forgiveness is a mistake. Ultimately, it is an absurdity.

As previously explained in this book (see chapter 6), my position is that, *technically*, there is no free will. If this is true, then the idea of forgiveness is based upon what I consider to be a very serious misunderstanding.

The need for forgiveness necessarily implies the belief that someone or something (whether apparently living or not) could have (technically, not theoretically) done something other than what they/it did, and that what they/it did was inherently and absolutely (as opposed to contextually and relatively) wrong.

After one fully understands, internalizes, and integrates an accurate understanding of the natural unfolding of the infinite and eternal flow of cause and effect at every scale, this view can only evoke deep tears of compassion for all who still hold to it and for all who interact with them.

Blame, shame, and guilt all rely upon the imaginary "gift" of free will in order to establish their validity. If nothing and no one could ever have done anything other than what it/he/she has done, is doing, and will do, then what is there to forgive?

Ironically, it seems quite likely that the idea of free will may have been invented and promoted so that common people could be controlled with blame, shame, and guilt. Where is the freedom in that? (I often find myself thinking of free will as the "gift" that keeps on *taking!*)

I want to strongly affirm my position that all of life, including every human being that has ever lived or will ever live, is absolutely and scientifically innocent.

Ultimately, there is only innocence!

What about accountability?

Accountability does *not* disappear along with the idea of free will, blame, shame, guilt, etc.

First, we are all part of the one universe and none can escape the natural flow of cause and effect.

Secondly, any time a society organizes itself at any level, "codes of conduct" begin to emerge that are (hopefully) originally intended to nurture the health and happiness of and for all (individually and collectively, including environment, etc.). Within such a society, accountability is entirely relevant, important, and not at all in conflict with the nature of nature (wherein technically free will does not exist). Rather, it is an expression of it!

This, however, does not mean that the members of any specific society will be endowed with any particular degree of wisdom in their creation and enforcement of such codes. And it should be emphatically stated that no good can result from making someone feel badly about their actions, no matter how heinous, even if they are asked/requested/obliged/forced to "make things right".

Now that I have brought up the idea of "right" and "wrong"...

I would like to suggest that "right" (aka "good") simply refers to that which nurtures greater well being; and "wrong" (aka "evil") simply refers to that which nurtures lesser well being. (For more information, please see Appendix III: Wholistic Ethics.) Of course, this kind of judgement depends upon the point of reference (the perspective of the one(s) making the judgement); the scale of self identity*; and the degree of intelligence, knowledge, and wisdom available and applied. *Among other things!*

I see "right" and "wrong" as entirely relevant and important (but largely misunderstood) judgements that have nothing to do with the inherent innocence or imaginary guilt of a person, place, or thing. Instead, I see the judgement of "right" and "wrong" as simply one's *best attempt* to determine whether the outcome(s) of a thought, decision, action, etc. will be (or were) more likely to nurture greater or lesser well being.

In my opinion, the world needs wise judgement, wise codes, and wise enforcement. *Systems, however, are unlikely to be wiser than their creators, and very likely to be significantly less!*

*As intimated in chapter 8, Earth, presently, makes a nice practical wholistic identity. Of course, considering how much space exploration we are doing and how much space trash we are creating, we really should start thinking about our *practical* wholistic identity as being our entire solar system. *Naturally, as our interaction, influence, and impact expands, our sense of wholistic identity will continue to expand.*

Chapter 13

THE KEY TO PREVENTION

Learn to Live in Continual Bliss

Some people are born into fortunate circumstances. The most fortunate of all circumstances is to have caretakers who are conscious, happy, and loving. In this case, serious energetic (emotional) injury is relatively unlikely.

Of course, many (perhaps most, in some places) people do not have caretakers who are truly conscious, happy, and loving. In these cases, serious energetic (emotional) injury is almost guaranteed.

Naturally, those who experience significant energetic (emotional) injuries early in life are far more likely to continue to experience a string of additional similar injuries as life goes along. Likewise, those who do not experience significant energetic (emotional) injuries early in life are far less likely to experience serious injuries later on. This is due to both practical and mystical reasons.

On the practical level:

Children learn by observing and modeling those around them. If they are surrounded by caretakers with negative beliefs and behaviors, they will very likely acquire these unhealthy beliefs, patterns, and habits from them. Obviously, positive and healthy beliefs, behaviors, etc. are transferred in the same way.

On the mystical level:

If a child begins life by learning from experience that life is unkind or even cruel (whether factually true or not) to him/her, then he/she will expect, and therefore attract, misfortune. And as misfortune is attracted and experienced, his/her faulty and negative (unhealthy) beliefs will naturally only be strengthened. Again, positive energy behaves in the very same way.

Fortunately, beliefs and behaviors can be questioned and changed. If the questions and changes are constructive, then the result will be ever-better life experiences. This will naturally reinforce one's beneficial beliefs (and likely create even more), which will naturally attract even better life experiences. *Ad infinitum.*

Of course, for those who have experienced significant energetic (emotional) injury, this process of constructively questioning and changing one's limiting and harmful beliefs and behaviors will naturally provoke and require a deep and complete personal healing (see chapter 12). This process can be quite challenging.

Therefore, if at all possible, I highly recommend living life (especially after investing in a deep and complete healing) in a way that will prevent further energetic injury (emotional damage) from occurring.

How is this done? I will now tell you, but be warned that you may not fully accept or appreciate my answer unless you have already begun your healing (again, see chapter 12) or are already living life in this, or in a very similar, way.

Simply put: Give up your demands, expectations, and (especially) requirements for happiness, and instead, practice the art of accepting and appreciating life *as it is!*

That being said, please do *not* give up your dreams, your desires, and your preferences for your own future life and for the future life of our beautiful planet! These are the very motivation of life itself and they are critical to experiencing ever-better experiences! (see chapter 14) The key is to make sure that these things don't become demands, expectations, and requirements for happiness.

It is of the highest importance that you realize that if you are experiencing any moment in a state of mind other than that of happiness (see chapter 11), then you are, in fact, injuring yourself. And this injury will become a candidate for later healing. Similarly, if you experience any moment in a state of true, conscious, and deep happiness, no injury can result and there will be no need for later healing related to that moment. Therefore, I suggest that you actively attempt to master the art of living every moment as happily as possible.

To this end, I would like to offer a personal living meditation that I have developed and used over the years while working with clients. It has proven to be extremely effective if undertaken seriously. Master it for yourself and then teach it to everyone you can - especially children! The sooner these habits are formed, the better life will be; both for the individual possessing them and for everyone around them!

SOREN'S LIVING MEDITATION
PART I: ACCEPTING AND APPRECIATING

Do your best to be totally present in every moment of your life. Be aware of what is true here and now, wherever and whenever you are. And also be aware of your desires for the near and/or long term future, because your desires are also part of what is true.

Then, be in a state of mind wherein you are absolutely committed to seeing, accepting, and allowing whatever you discover to be true, to be true. You don't have to be (and can't truly be) happy about the things that you are not happy about, but realize and practice the wisdom of accepting the truth as it is and allowing it to be as it is.

Make sure that you really do want to see and know the truth. Make sure that you really are committed to honoring the truth by accepting it as the truth. Make sure that you really do feel a state of allowing it to be as it is so that there is not a trace of resistance within you.

Then, attempt to make the very best and the very most of each and every moment by simultaneously:

1) Accepting and allowing all that is true to be true

2) Appreciating everything you can about what is true

3) Actively nurturing the manifestation of whatever you would prefer to be true in the near and/or long term future

That's it!

Of course, I do fully realize that living every moment in this way is much easier said than done. Nonetheless, if you will practice this living meditation long enough, then you will eventually discover that you can, in fact, allow yourself to be supremely happy *simply because you can!*

Ultimately, you are the judge and jury of your own happiness; so, if possible, lower your own requirements for happiness until there is only *the requirement of existing!*

"I exist, therefore I am perfectly happy!"

"I allow and experience enduring ecstasy!"

Chapter 14

THE KEY TO CREATION

How Great Can Your Life Be?

If the truth cannot be changed, then where is the wisdom in resisting it? As previously established, there is none! There is, however, great wisdom in being resistless to the truth while *simultaneously* remaining aware of your personal preferences for the not yet manifested future. Personal preferences, however, are not demands placed upon the universe. Nor are they requirements for happiness. Unfortunately, such requirements and demands are often born of them.

I suggest replacing your demands and requirements with a deep desire to answer, with your very life itself, the most powerful question of all: "How great can life be?"

If we all consciously shared this desire as our highest individual and collective mission in life, we would transform our individual and collective worlds so fast that it would blow our own, as well as our ancestors', minds! Our descendants, on the other hand, would most likely see our phoenix-like transformation as completely natural, perhaps even unavoidable. Of course, they would probably also express deep and profound gratitude for the fact that we became conscious of the truth and aligned to it before we destroyed ourselves in ignorance and greed!

The truth is that we currently have *extremely* powerful communication and technology systems - far more than is needed for radical and rapid planetary transformation. The missing ingredient is simply the conscious and harmonious alignment of individual and collective human desire until it becomes our highest common intention to answer, with our very lives, the most powerful question of all: "How great can life be?"

Naturally, the question, "How great can life be?", will give birth to other powerful supporting questions such as, "How great can this moment be?" or "How great can my health be?" or "How great can this relationship be?" or "How great can this opportunity be?". All of these questions are significant and worthy as long as they *truly* consciously serve the original question/intention/desire.

However, if a question arises (and is nurtured) that does not truly serve a health and happiness nurturing question/intention/desire, then trouble is sure to follow. For instance, a question that is fueled primarily by curiosity and greed such as, "How much money, power, etc. can I acquire?" returns an answer that comes in the form of a death sentence. (*I have plenty more to say about this, but I am sure that I would only be preaching to the choir!*)

Whether conscious or not, putting yourself in the service of a specific desire is an incredibly powerful thing to do! In every moment, we use our emotions, our thoughts, our words, and our actions to create our world. *Let's consciously decide to make it an ever-better one!*

Ours are the hands of God. Ours is the voice of God. Ours are the ears and the eyes of God. Ours is the mind of God. And ours is the heart of God. As many have rightly said, "We are the ones we have been waiting for."

With that in mind, I'd like to share with you a very powerful way to influence the nature of emerging reality.

SOREN'S LIVING MEDITATION
PART II: CREATING YOUR REALITY

Do your best to make sure that you feel no resistance to the truth, and therefore enjoy a relatively constant state of inner peace (see Part I of the Living Meditation, found in chapter 13). From this place you can cause very powerful positive changes in your own life and in the world around you. Here are a few simple steps to guide you until this process becomes habitual.

First, remember your fundamental intention to be and live in a happy state of mind. Remember your intention to recognize, appreciate, and amplify the greatness in every moment. Remember your intention to find out how great this moment, the future, and life in general can be. REMEMBER. REMEMBER. REMEMBER.

1) Know exactly what effect you want to cause (your ultimate intention), and personally commit to doing whatever is required for as long as is required in order to nurture that manifestation, even if it requires the rest of your life. *And, of course, choose your intentions wisely!*

2) In whatever way seems most appropriate and powerful to you, formally invite the entire universe to help you. For many people this begins as a private meditation or prayer, but it can also be a publicly spoken or written request.

3) Do everything you can every day to contribute to and nurture the effect that you desire. For best results, your thoughts, words, and actions should be ethical, effective, efficient, and enjoyable. For even better results, *always follow your intuition* whether it makes sense to your conscious mind or not. The more you accept, allow, and trust life, the more strongly you will be guided by a still small voice from within. Perhaps this is the voice of life itself. Perhaps it is your own innermost voice. Perhaps there is no difference. In any event, *trust it!*

4) Authentically recognize and appreciate everything that nurtures you, your happiness, and the effect that you desire.

5) If, at any point, you find that you are not presently in a state of authentic happiness (in other words, you have any difficulty accepting anything that is true), reread the parts of this book that seem most relevant to you, especially the Healing Meditation and Part I of the Living Meditation.

In summary, stay awake, stay present, and meet every moment with the commitment to make the very best and very most of everything. In every moment, simultaneously accept and allow all that is true to be true, while actively nurturing the manifestation of your preferred future.

Constantly ask yourself the question: "How can I (not how *could* I, but how *can* I) make this moment even better for myself and for those around me?" And always seek to answer, with your very life itself, the most powerful question of all: "How great can life be?"

It's your life! Make it an ever-better one!

()

Chapter 15

SUMMARIZING
SPIRITUALITY

To Live as though We are One

So, then, what *exactly* does it mean to be spiritual?

People seem to make this question much more difficult and complicated than is necessary. Given the profound amount of destruction that has taken place in the name of God, religion, and so-called spirituality, it is quite understandable. Therefore, I would like to request that you set aside, if you haven't already done so, all of your previous thoughts and feelings about spirituality just long enough to seriously consider what I have to say.

In my opinion, to be consciously spiritual is to *know* that we are one and to think, speak, and act accordingly. *Unconditional love is the sign of true spirituality!*

And the gifts of spiritual realization (to know that we are one) and dedication (to think, speak, and act accordingly) are many. Among the most noteworthy spiritual gifts are: inner peace, intuition, and a significantly increased ability to manifest one's desires.

It seems to me that spirituality is the natural result of genuine intelligence and true knowledge, just as *wisdom* is. In fact, spirituality is a symptom of wisdom. Where you find *true* spirituality, you will surely find wisdom!

As I end this chapter, I feel intuitively guided to issue a somewhat veiled warning in the form of a personal suggestion and appeal for your own spiritual awakening:

Sit quietly with yourself and with nature. Listen carefully to your innermost self and to nature. Trust your innermost self and trust nature. And question every human word and human action. Do not value other's insight and guidance more than your own unless you have an *extremely* good reason to do so. And do not trust anyone who does not support this advice. *This is especially important at this particular time in history!*

Conclusion

WHERE IS THE WISDOM?

So, then, where *exactly* is the wisdom?

It is within you and it is all around you. If you take the time to listen carefully to the subtle voice of truth within you, then you will begin to hear the quiet, yet firm, proclamations of wisdom. And if you pay close attention to the words and actions of those around you, then you will begin to recognize those who are already well tuned in to the truth and to that which will generally nurture the health and happiness of all that is.

Wisdom is also hiding in plain site wherever indigenous people still live in and with *nature*. In fact, there seems to be a strong correlation between nature and wisdom, just as there seems to be between nature and spirituality.

Wisdom is also especially present in the places where it appears to have been intentionally hidden and protected, such as the high mountain temples of India and (until recently) Tibet (unfortunately Tibet's protections were/ are no match for modern ambitions and agendas).

Wisdom is also well infused, if sometimes distorted and/or misunderstood, in the fundamental teachings of *every authentic religion!*

Unfortunately, wisdom is *not* present within many religious leaders. Just as many of our governments have historically been hi-jacked by undisclosed and unwise special interest groups, so have many of our religions. *This point is of critical and intentionally understated importance!*

If you belong to any kind of organization (business, government, religion, church, social cause, rock band, street gang, whatever, etc.) that has a leader that lacks wisdom and integrity, then kindly ask him/her to step down and actively help select someone else that you feel is better qualified. Or, if you prefer, simply leave the organization and find, or start, another one that you believe is *led by wisdom towards an ever-better world!*

Let's not allow the preciousness that life on Earth *is* to be devastated by leadership that lacks wisdom. Let's not allow our awesome opportunity to make the best and the most of life on Earth (and beyond!) to be wasted.

Instead, let us be, find, and follow wisdom!

We can do better than this! We can love more, we can enjoy more, and we can create an ever-better world!

Just how great can life be?

Let's find out!

APPENDICES

APPENDIX I

THE CENTER FOR
SPIRITUAL ATHEISM

Gardening on the World Wide Web

In 2004, I built the first version of *The Center for Spiritual Atheism* web site (www.SpiritualAtheism.com). I felt that there was a previously unidentified and unnamed group of people who were not strictly atheists, theists, or agnostics. I theorized that there were a significant number of people who, categorically, did not believe in the existence of God as understood and presented by traditional theists; and yet they knew that all is one and that this wholeness is the very thing that the symbolic reference, God, refers to. I imagined a vast ocean of spiritually awake and spiritually literate people who were teeming with wisdom and waiting anxiously for an invitation to come together and consciously help to create an ever-better world. *I am still holding this vision!*

It was my intention to gradually (informally) unify all self-identified "spiritual atheists", regardless of their *particular* philosophies and points of view. But there was actually more to it than this. You see, I had been asking myself a very powerful question for many years prior. That question was, "What is the most powerful thing that *I* can do to *help* create a better world?" The answer that I finally settled on was to *help* destroy spiritual illiteracy (the inability to recognize spiritual symbols as such).

It seemed to me that spiritual illiteracy was not only the ultimate cause of conflict between different spiritual traditions and positions, but even more significantly, it seemed to me to be the very reason that *wholistically unhealthy* agendas have been able to flourish over the centuries virtually unrecognized and unchallenged by the easily distracted, divided, and demoralized masses.

I also concluded that the most powerful way to destroy this ignorance (spiritual illiteracy) was to prove to irrational atheists that God does exist (as the universe) and to prove to irrational theists that God does not exist (as a white-bearded wizard); it is simply a matter of perspective.

If I could be successful, it would mean that these divisions (theist and atheist) would cease to be meaningful. Likewise, when the term "spiritual atheism" reaches full maturity, it will also no longer have any real practical value - except perhaps historical! In my opinion, that day can't come soon enough!

And so it was that I planted a conscious and intentional seed in the fertile soil of our online world. Since that time it has grown exponentially and has given birth to many other projects including *The Center for a Better World* (www.CenterForABetterWorld.com) and *The Alliance for a Better World* (www.AllianceForABetterWorld.com).

May these projects (and all other similar projects nurtured by others) continue to grow and eventually produce all of the fruits of peace, love, joy, and abundance that I (and so many others) continue to dream of and work towards!

APPENDIX II

UNIVERSAL SPIRITUALITY

As presented at: www.CenterForABetterWorld.com

*Do you recognize the intrinsic infinite
"connectedness" and "oneness" of all things?*

*Have you decided to live in a way that nurtures
the health and happiness of all things?*

It seems that all sincere truth-seekers eventually conclude that the word "God" was probably not originally intended to refer to a fictitious white-bearded wizard who lives just outside of the known universe, but rather, to the infinite and eternal universe itself.

*Is God's body not the very universe itself? Is God's consciousness not the
very consciousness that is present in all of life everywhere?
Is not all of life sacred?*

That the human family is a *conscious and able* aspect of the universe is *significant!* It means that we have the extraordinary opportunity to consciously make a substantial contribution to the well-being of all that exists within our ever-expanding sphere of awareness and influence (which is presently generally represented by Earth).

Unfortunately, there are still many members of our human family who don't recognize the ancient *spiritual symbols* (such as "God", "self", "good", and "evil") as such. The result is not only a devastating division of our human family, it is also a devastating decimation of the very natural resources that make continued human life possible!

However, if we can eradicate *spiritual illiteracy*, we will liberate an astounding number of intelligent and creative people who will naturally want to help to create a better world.

Literal religions have been allowed to disable and divide people for far too long. It is time for all who understand the problem *and the solution* to stand up and speak out.

True "spirituality" has *absolutely nothing* to do with adopting a specific religion or believing in a fictitious God. Instead, it is the natural result of realizing that the entire universe is connected, if only by the mystical flow of cause and effect *at every scale.*

Truly spiritual beings realize that as we go about our lives striving to be healthy and happy, we should also be striving to help the world around us to be healthy and happy.

Of course, spirituality ultimately means far more than simply living according to *what should be* common-sense ethics; it also means balancing one's limited sense of self, self-knowing, self-guidance, etc. with one's mystical relationship to the infinite universe.

To the extent that one is successful in balancing one's own finite identity and significance with one's infinite identity and significance, one will be overcome by authentic and unconditional love. Love of *all* that is, *all* that has ever been, and *all* that will ever be.

Love is the true sign of true spirituality.
And love is the key to a better world!

WHOLISTIC ETHICS

As presented at: www.CenterForABetterWorld.com

Naturally, we all want to be as healthy and as happy as possible.

A careful observation of the universe reveals that:

1) All parts of space can be viewed as both an individual part of a larger system as well as a collective system of smaller individual parts. Ultimately, all of space is revealed to be one infinitely large system made up of infinitely small parts.

APPLICATION: On a practical level, this naturally suggests that an ideal guiding perspective is one that balances the importance of the well-being of the individuals with the importance of the well-being of the collectives.

2) All events of time can be viewed as both a set of effects as well as a set of causes. Ultimately, all of time is revealed to be one eternal chain of causes and effects.

APPLICATION: On a practical level, this naturally suggests that an ideal guiding perspective is one that balances the importance of appreciating present well-being with the importance of nurturing future well-being.

Since we are one infinite entity that is eternally bound to an infinite chain of causes and effects, we can most effectively and efficiently experience ever-greater well-being by spending our time, money, and all other resources in the following balanced way:

1) Enjoying one's own present well-being
2) Helping others to enjoy their present well-being
3) Nurturing one's own future well-being
4) Helping others to nurture their future well-being

This wisdom naturally reveals an objective, scientific, spiritual, and universal system of ethics which suggests that an unbalanced (in the terms outlined above) expenditure of time, money, and all other resources that favors any of the above aspects of our infinite and eternal existence, *especially at the expense of any of the others*, is not preferred (aka "wrong"), as it is harmful (aka "evil"); while a **balanced** expenditure of time, money, and all other resources **is preferred** (aka "right"), as it is helpful (aka "good").

In other words, that which is "right" or "good" is that which leads to greater well-being, while that which is "wrong" or "evil" is that which leads to lesser well-being. The critical key to accurate judgement is the recognition that, ultimately, we are all one infinite and eternal entity, and therefore, our well-being is the natural result of successfully balancing our sense of priority between the dynamics of space(individual/self and collective/others) and time (now and future).

I call this simple, sensible, and powerful system of ethics, "Wholistic Ethics". Using this universal system of ethics as our moral compass, we can easily discern the difference between that which is helpful and that which is harmful to the well-being of our world as a whole, and ultimately, unite around sound judgements and plans of action regardless of our spiritual, political, national, or racial affiliations. Under these conditions, we can move swiftly from a dying world to a *thriving world.*

Additional note: Many people promote the idea that "good" and "evil" are merely polarized opposites that balance the whole (ultimately suggesting equal desirability); but, in my opinion, this widespread belief is extremely dangerous to our wholistic health and happiness. If you hold this belief, I strongly urge you to seriously consider the proposition that "good" *is* balance and that "evil" *is* imbalance. *I think you will find this perspective to be very revealing!*

APPENDIX IV

THE CENTER
FOR A BETTER WORLD
Inspiring, Empowering, and Uniting Humanity

Our precious world is composed of many different races, nations, political affiliations, religious affiliations, and philosophical perspectives. Despite all of our differences, we all share the transcendent desire to be happy and to live in a universally happy world.

This kind of happiness is possible!

I created the Center for a Better World web site (*www.CenterForABetterWorld.com*) in 2005. Ultimately, it is my intention to create an organization (the Center) that is dedicated to inspiring, empowering, and (informally) uniting our human family (the Alliance) to *help* create an ever-better world as ethically, effectively, efficiently, and enjoyably as possible. For various reasons, this project has been very slow to develop, but I patiently maintain this grand vision and invite you to step forward and *help* to create it.

The basic idea is that the best way to create an ever-better world is to first intend to do so. After that, we can begin the work, all the while improving the method by which we determine and do the work.

I see the "Center" as an organization (with appropriate resources) that *serves* all who intend to actively help create an ever-better world (the "Alliance"). Although I have some partially developed ideas, I don't claim to know how the Center can *best* serve the Alliance. In fact, I don't think any one person can know such things. That being said, I believe that, together, we can create ever-better answers to this and any other question that arises. *And we would be well served to create ever-better questions too!*

The current state of the Center is based upon my limited questions, answers, time and other resources. Naturally, it can become *infinitely more* by integrating others' questions, answers, time and other resources.

Where is our world's greatest wisdom, intelligence, and creativity?

The Center for a Better World is searching for the brightest minds and purest hearts from all around the world. For more information about sponsorship, collaboration, employment, internship, and volunteer opportunities; please join the Alliance for a Better World community (www.AllianceForABetterWorld.com); visit our web site in order to review our current projects and apparent needs (www.CenterForABetterWorld.com); and let us know about your specific interests and potential contributions. *Established leaders are also encouraged to join us!*

Also note that many sections of our web sites are not (as of mid 2012) as functional or attractive as we would like them to be. In fact, we have been developing a fantastic vision for a next-generation social networking environment that is both intentional and fun! If you, or someone you know, would like to be part of this exciting new project, please let us know. Programmers and philanthropists are especially encouraged to contact us.

THE CENTER FOR A BETTER WORLD

OUR MISSION STATEMENT

To *help* create a better world by inspiring, empowering, and uniting our human family to *help* create an ever-better world as ethically, effectively, efficiently, and enjoyably as possible.

OUR EIGHT EMPOWERING INTENTIONS

COMMUNITY DEVELOPMENT

1) To Improve Our Organization (The Center)
2) To Nurture Our Community (The Alliance)

PHILOSOPHICAL IMPROVEMENT

4) To Nurture Wholistic Ethics (see Appendix III)
3) To Nurture Universal Spirituality (see Appendix II)

PSYCHOLOGICAL IMPROVEMENT

5) To Nurture the Empowerment of Individuals
6) To Nurture the Empowerment of Organizations

GUARDIANSHIP AND STEWARDSHIP

7) To Nurture the Protection and Support
of Those Who Need It
8) To Nurture the Protection and Rehabilitation
   of Our Environment

APPENDIX V

THE ALLIANCE
FOR A BETTER WORLD
Working Together for One and All

Every thought, feeling, decision, word, and action adds to, or detracts from, the health and happiness of the world. Therefore, every moment should be recognized as a valuable opportunity to *help* create a better world.

**You exist at the very center of decision and action.
You exist at the very center of a better world.**

The moment you consciously decide to help create a better world, you instantly and automatically become an extremely valuable member of the Alliance for a Better World. There is no membership application or formal obligation; there is only your personal decision to help as you are able. *Welcome to the Alliance!*

Our world is teeming with intelligence and wisdom!

If you would like to meet other people who have also consciously decided to help create a better world, you are invited to visit *www.AllianceForABetterWorld.com*. Not only can you meet other like-minded people, you can share your specific intentions and visions and ask for the help you need while exploring opportunities to help others materialize their visions. *Come and help to create a better world!*

Let's do this thing!

A FINAL NOTE

If you like what I have said, but feel an inner urge to offer a correction, addition, enhancement, or other improvement, I invite you to contact me with your constructive suggestions. I also welcome your collaborative book, film, web site, and/or other related project proposals. *Especially if they involve plenty of fun!*

BOOKS BY SOREN SORENSEN

A Book That Could Change the World
Confessions of a Spiritual Atheist

This magickal book presents a progressive series of simple, yet cryptic, confessions (beliefs) that are each accompanied by a playful and symbolic illustration. Each idea invites an intriguing inquiry into the beliefs, assumptions, and attitudes that shape your life experiences; causing an ever-greater expansion of consciousness and intention that is sure to change your world, and the world around you, *for the better!*

Spiritual Atheism
The Way of Wisdom

Spiritual Atheism is no oxymoron. It is the key to your happiness. And it is the key to a better world. This book will challenge you to reconsider your foundational philosophical assumptions about the nature of existence, identity, motivation, happiness, healing, forgiveness, consciousness, creation, intention, and manifestation from a shockingly direct and extremely powerful point of view. Discover a radical, inspiring, and liberating way to understand your life and live it to its *fullest potential!*

For more information about these and other forthcoming books, visit: www.SpiritualAtheist.com

ABOUT THE AUTHOR

SOREN SORENSEN

Soren has been serving as a professional spiritual counselor, healer, teacher, and life coach since 2005, after leaving his successful 10 year career as a systems analyst. He chose to make "helping people" the central focus of the next phase of his life's work after receiving overwhelming feedback from co-workers and friends that his insights, questions, and suggestions were changing their lives.

Soren has the rare ability to guide his clients on a direct and compassionate exploration of their personal life experiences that quickly shatters the illusions that are keeping them from their own happiness and power to create positive changes in their own lives and in the world around them.

Like many natural philosophers before him, Soren has been fascinated by the nature of existence since early childhood, and he continues to refine his perspective through careful observation, meditation, and experimentation.

As of 2012, Soren lives "off the grid" in an experimental "micro-home" with his equally inspiring wife, Grace.

For more information about Soren, visit:
www.SorenSorensen.com